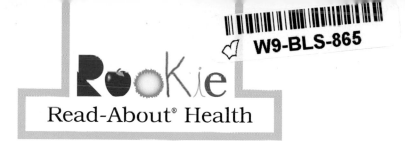

W9-BLS-865

Read-About® Health

Hearing

By Sharon Gordon

Consultants
Nanci R. Vargus, Ed.D.
Primary Multiage Teacher
Decatur Township Schools, Indianapolis, Indiana

Jan Jenner, Ph.D.

SCHOLASTIC INC.
New York Toronto London Auckland Sydney
Mexico City New Delhi Hong Kong Buenos Aires

Designer: Herman Adler Design
Photo Researcher: Caroline Anderson
The photo on the cover shows a young boy cupping his ear to hear better.

ISBN 0-516-24512-0

12 11 10 9 8 7 6 5 4 3 2 1   2 3 4 5 6 7/0

Printed in the U.S.A.   61

First Scholastic paperback printing, September 2002

Listen! Do you hear that?

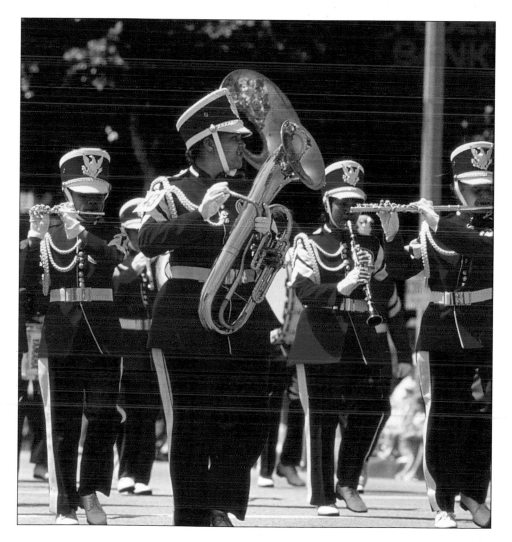

Hearing is one of the five senses. The other senses are seeing, touching, smelling, and tasting.

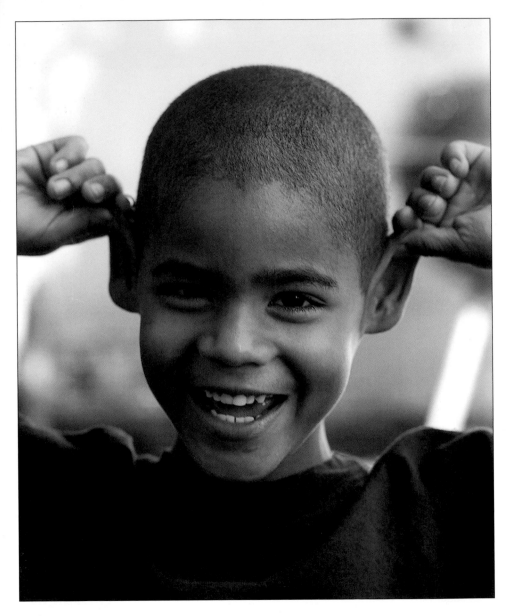

You hear with your ears.

You have one ear on each side of your head. This helps you hear things all around you.

Look in a mirror.

You can only see part
of your ear. That part
is called the outer ear.

The outer ear is shaped
like a baseball glove.
It *catches* the sounds
around you.

The sounds go into the
little hole in your ear.
They move through a tube
into your middle ear.

Brain

Outer Ear

Inner Ear

14

The sounds keep moving
until they reach your
inner car. The inner ear
sends them to your brain.

That is how you hear things.

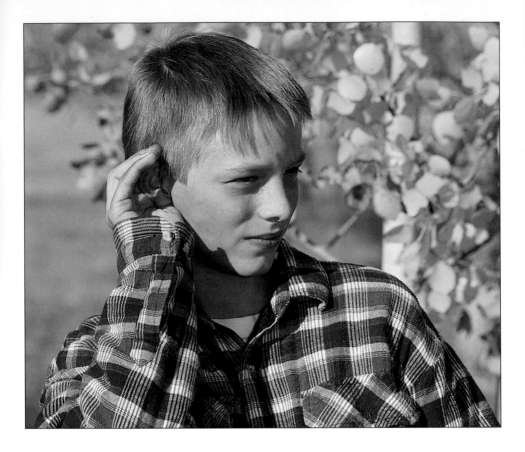

If a sound is too soft, you
can cup your hands around
your ears to hear it better.

So that's what you heard!

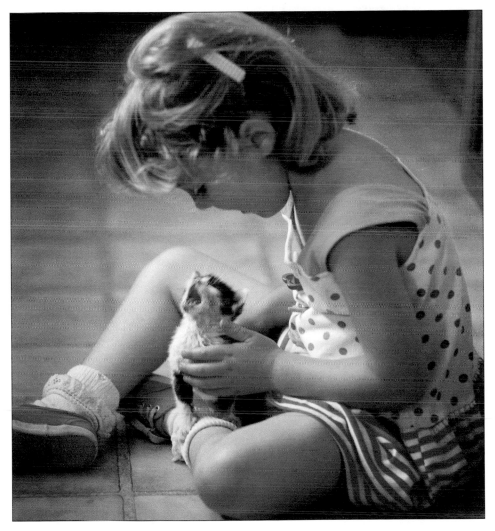

You can cover your ears
if a sound is too loud.

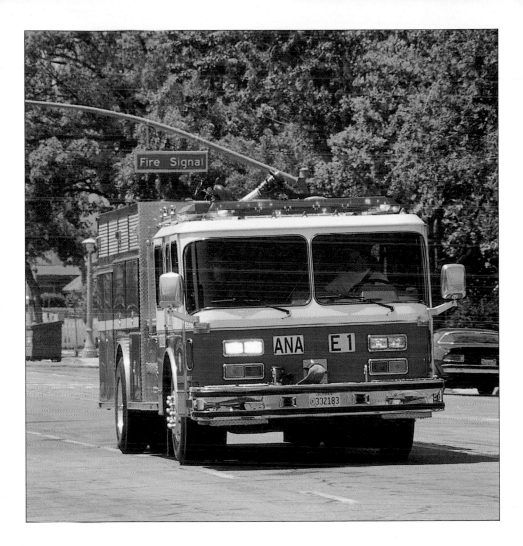

Here comes the fire engine!

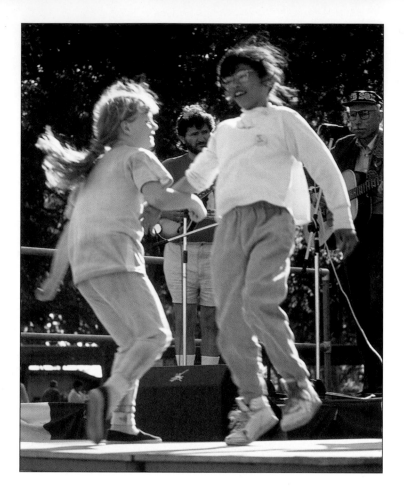

Some sounds make
you want to dance.

Others make you want to clap your hands.

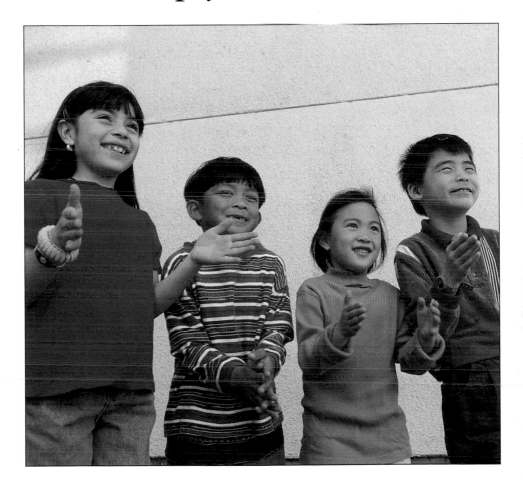

There are sounds that
can wake you up.

24

There are sounds that can put you to sleep.

Some sounds are high, like a whistle.

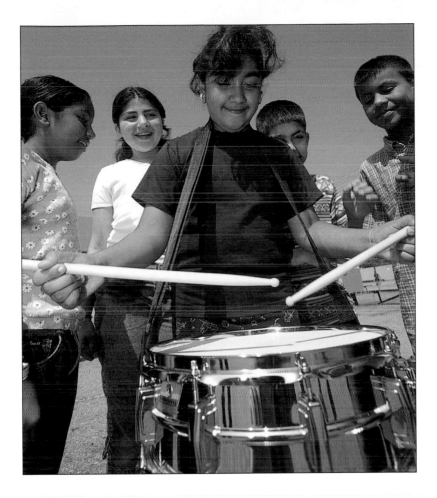

Some sounds are low,
like a drum.

And some sounds
are just plain fun.

Surprise!

Words You Know

baseball glove

brain

drum

outer ear

sounds

whistle

Index

About the Author

Sharon Gordon is a writer living in Midland Park, New Jersey. She and her husband have three school-aged children and a spoiled pooch. Together they enjoy visiting the Outer Banks of North Carolina as often as possible.

Photo Credits

Photographs ©: Corbis-Bettmann: 17, 31 bottom left (Brian Leng), 26, 31 bottom right (Wartenberg Picture Press), 24 (Doug Wilson); Mandy Rosenfeld: 18; Photo Researchers, NY: 10 left (Ken Cavanagh), 13, 31 top (Richard Hutchings); PhotoEdit: 3 (Gary Conner), 23 (Laura Dwight), 19 (Tony Freeman), 21, 27, 30 bottom right (Michael Newman), 16 (Mary Steinbacher), 20 (David Young-Wolff); Rigoberto Quinteros: 5, 6, 10 right, 30 top; Stone: 29 (Arthur Tilley); Visuals Unlimited: cover, 9 (Eric Anderson).

Illustration by Patricia Rasch.